MARTIN LUTHER KING

CIVIL RIGHTS ACTIVIST

Jen Green

Published in paperback in 2014 by
Wayland
Copyright © Wayland 2014

Wayland
338 Euston Road
London NW1 3BH

Wayland Australia
Level 17/207 Kent Street
Sydney, NSW 2000

Editor: Elizabeth Brent
Design: Basement68
Picture Research: Shelley Noronha

British Library Cataloguing in
Publication Data
Green, Jen.
Martin Luther King. -- (Inspirational lives)
 1. King, Martin Luther, Jr.,
1929–1968--Juvenile literature.
 2. African American civil rights workers--
Biography--Juvenile literature.
I. Title II. Series
323.1'196'073'092-dc23

ISBN: 978 0 7502 8352 6

10 9 8 7 6 5 4 3 2 1

Printed in China

Wayland is a division of
Hachette Children's Books,
an Hachette UK company.

www.hachette.co.uk

Picture acknowledgments: The author
and publisher would like to thank the
following for allowing their pictures
to be reproduced in this publication:
Cover: © Popperfoto/Getty Images; p4
© The Granger Collection/TopFoto; p5 ©
AFP/Getty Images; p6 © Getty Images;
p7 © JTB/Photoshot; p8 © Topham
Picturepoint; p9 © Getty Images (l),
Topham Picturepoint (r); p10 © Alex and
Anna/Shutterstock.com; p11 © Epic/Mary
Evans Picture Library; p12 © Michael Ochs
Archives/Getty Images; p13 © The Image
Works/TopFoto; p14 © Bettmann/Corbis;
p15 © Bettmann/Corbis; p16 © TopFoto;
p17 © Getty Images; p18 © Topham
Picturepoint; p19 © Time & Life Pictures/
Getty Images; p20 © Topham/AP; p21 ©
Flip Schulke/Corbis; p22 © Bettmann/
Corbis; p23 © Time & Life Pictures/Getty
Images; p24 © AFP/Getty Images; p25 ©
Getty Images; p26 © Popperfoto/Getty
Images; p27 © AFP/Getty Images; p28
© TIPS/Photoshot; p29 © Mesut Dogan/
Shutterstock.com

Contents

I have a dream

On a hot August day in 1963, a black clergyman prepares to address a huge crowd. Martin Luther King Junior (Jr) looks out over the sea of faces gathered in Washington DC, the American capital. The TV cameras are whirring. He has just minutes to inspire the crowd, and to convince the world about what he believes in. The only problem is, he hasn't decided exactly what to say.

In the 1960s, American society was not equal. **Prejudice** against black people was common, especially in southern America. Martin Luther King Jr was the last speaker at a huge demonstration aimed at improving conditions for black people and other **minorities**.

Thousands of people had travelled to Washington to campaign for equality and an end to **discrimination** on the grounds of race.

Martin Luther King Jr spent his life campaigning peacefully to change society. Non-violence was essential to his cause.

INSPIRATION

Martin Luther King Jr's 'I have a dream' speech is widely seen as one of the most famous speeches ever given. Martin's words were simple, beautiful and yet challenging. Rather than focusing on the details of the current campaign, he presented a vision of the future that gave people something to hope and aim for.

Martin had prepared a speech but, at the last minute, he decided to put his notes away and speak from the heart. He presented his vision of a society free from prejudice. He spoke of the day when all Americans would be truly equal. 'I have a dream that my four little children will one day live in a nation where they will not be judged by the color of their skin but by the content of their character. I have a dream today.'

When Martin had finished speaking there was complete silence. Then everyone started to cheer and clap. His words gave African Americans the pride and courage they needed in the fight for equality. Martin's vision still inspires many people today.

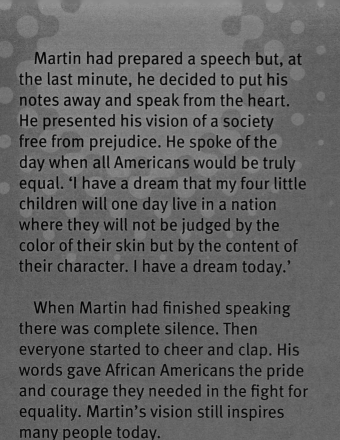

WOW!

Martin Luther King Jr campaigned for weeks to persuade people to join the demonstration – in the end there were 250,000 demonstrators, including 60,000 white people.

*Martin Luther King Jr's speech is seen as a key moment in the fight for **civil rights**.*

Early life

Martin Luther King Jr was born in 1929, the second child of Martin Luther King Senior (Snr) and his wife Alberta. Martin Jr grew up in a well-to-do, loving family. Yet from an early age, he was aware of the hardship and poverty experienced by most African Americans around him.

Martin Snr was the minister of Ebenezer Baptist Church in Atlanta, Georgia. Atlanta lay in the heart of southern USA, where prejudice against black Americans was widespread. Throughout the South, a series of state, city and local laws made African Americans into second-class citizens. These laws enforced **segregation** – the separation of black and white people in schools and public places such as restaurants. Black people had to use the back entrance to shops and cinemas, and were not allowed in whites-only parks. These **racist** laws were known as the Jim Crow laws.

A young girl leaves a segregated cafe in southern USA in 1950.

INSPIRATION

Once when Martin was little, he was riding in his father's car when Martin Snr was stopped by a white policeman, who called him 'boy'. The preacher stood up for himself. Pointing to Martin, he said: 'That is a boy. I am a man.' Martin never forgot his father's courage.

Martin's father believed that segregation was wrong. He was active in a group called the National Association for the Advancement of Colored People (NAACP). This was the first organisation to campaign for black civil rights in America.

Martin Jr was a clever boy. From a young age he could recite whole passages from the Bible by heart. He also liked baseball, riding his bike and playing with model planes.

Martin had his first taste of **racism** at the age of six. He was forbidden to play with two white boys who lived nearby by the boys' mother, because he was black. Martin's parents explained about discrimination. But his mother said: 'Never feel you are less than anybody else.'

WOW!

Martin was a sensitive child who took things to heart. He was out watching a parade when his beloved grandmother died. When he found out, he felt so guilty about not being at her bedside that he threw himself out of an upstairs window and bruised himself badly.

Martin grew up with his sister, Christine, and brother, Albert Daniel, in this two-storey house near his father's church. The Kings were well-off at a time when a great many people were poor and jobless.

A gifted pupil, Martin did well at school. He enjoyed all sorts of music and played the violin. As a teenager he dressed smartly and was good at dancing, which made him popular with girls. But not even a happy childhood could shield him from the discrimination that black people faced in the South.

Martin became interested in public speaking. At 14 he took part in a state-wide debating competition, and travelled to a town 145 km (90 miles) away to take part in the final. His speech on 'The Negro and the Constitution' won first prize. But on the bus ride home, the driver ordered him and his teacher to stand so that white people could sit down. This rule was an example of the petty discrimination of the Jim Crow laws. Martin later said that this incident made him 'the angriest I have ever been in my life'. The young man resolved to do something to change the way that black people were treated when he grew up.

The Ku Klux Klan was a secret society made up of white racists opposed to improving conditions for black people. Klan members hid their identity by wearing white robes with hoods.

WOW!

Martin was a bright pupil. He jumped a couple of grades at school and started high school in 1942, at the age of 13. There he continued to do well, coming top in English and history.

Racial prejudice in the South had its roots in slavery. From the early 1500s to the 1800s, 11–12 million Africans were captured and shipped to the Americas to live and work as slaves. There they were very badly treated, denied an education and forced to live in terrible conditions. In 1776 the United States won its independence from Britain, and the slave trade was abolished. But slavery continued in the South.

In 1861 civil war broke out in America between North and South because the southern states refused to end slavery. In 1865 the South was defeated and all black slaves were freed. But racism and discrimination remained part of life in the South. In the late 1800s the Jim Crow laws introduced segregation in public places and reduced the rights of black people, making it more difficult for them to vote.

INSPIRATION

In 1944 Martin spent the summer working on a farm in Connecticut in northeastern America. Here he enjoyed his first taste of a society in which black people were allowed into the same shops and restaurants as white people. After a summer of freedom, it was hard to return to segregation in the South.

The picture on the left shows a slave family in South Carolina in 1862. The poster on the right is from 1829, and is advertising a slave auction.

Training to be a minister

At 15 Martin finished high school, but this was not the end of his studies. In September 1944 he started at Morehouse College in Atlanta. The college was taking underage students because this was the time of World War II, and many young men were away fighting.

Martin Snr had studied at Morehouse, but at first, Martin did not want to become a preacher like his father. He was thinking of becoming a doctor or a lawyer. However, the Morehouse principal persuaded him that entering the Church was the best choice if he wanted to work for social change. In 1947 he gave a trial sermon at his father's church. He was **ordained** as a minister the following year, at just 19 years old.

This map shows the Southern states of America, where segregation was practised.

After graduating from Morehouse, Martin went to Crozer Theological Seminary in Chester, Pennsylvania, to study for a BA in **Divinity**. This college was in the North. There Martin studied philosophers such as Henry David Thoreau. From Crozer he went on to study for a doctorate at Boston University, Massachusetts.

Life was not all study. Martin dated a number of girls before meeting a music student called Coretta Scott. On their very first date, Martin told Coretta she had all the qualities he wished for in a wife: character, intelligence, personality and beauty. The couple were married by Martin's father in June 1953.

As Martin's studies ended he began looking for a job as a minister. He was offered a post at Dexter Avenue Baptist Church in Montgomery, Alabama. The job involved moving back to the South and segregation, but Martin decided his place was there, campaigning to improve the lives of black people.

Martin and Coretta as newlyweds, 18 June 1953.

INSPIRATION

At college Martin read the works of American writer Henry David Thoreau (1817–62). Thoreau believed in following his conscience. He argued it was right to disobey the state if its laws were unjust. Thoreau refused to pay taxes to a country that supported slavery, and went to jail for it. This form of protest is called **civil disobedience**. Thoreau also influenced the Indian leader Mahatma Gandhi (see page 17).

The Montgomery bus protest

In 1955, an incident on a bus in Martin's new home, Montgomery, sparked the start of the civil rights movement across America. It also shot the young preacher to fame, at the age of just 26.

Martin spent most of 1954 settling into his new role as a preacher. He worked hard on his sermons, trying to attract a wide range of people to his church. He was also becoming more active in black politics. He was made a leader of the Montgomery branch of the NAACP. In 1955, he and Coretta were delighted with the birth of their first child, a baby girl called Yolanda.

Martin's speech on the eve of the bus protest is widely seen as marking the start of the civil rights movement.

In 1954, the US Supreme Court ruled that segregation in public schools was **illegal**. This gave the black **community** hope for the future. But in Montgomery, segregation was still in force in public places and on public transport. On the city buses the rule was that white people sat in the front, with African Americans in the rear seats. Black people could only sit in the middle rows if no white person wanted to sit there.

On 1 December 1955, a black **seamstress** named Rosa Parks refused to give up her seat on the bus to a white person. She was arrested. Martin met with other black leaders and decided to launch a campaign to support Rosa. They asked black people to **boycott** the buses until the racist law was changed.

Martin's house lay on a bus route. The following morning he and Coretta watched as bus after bus drove past with no one on board. The boycott was working!

INSPIRATION

At the first bus campaign meeting, Martin gave a stirring speech. 'There comes a time when people get tired... tired of being segregated and humiliated. We are not wrong in what we are doing. If we are wrong, the Constitution of the United States is wrong. If we are wrong, God Almighty is wrong... If we are wrong, justice is a lie.'

Rosa Parks being fingerprinted by a white policeman, 1955.

TOP TIP

Speech-makers often use repetition to underline their argument. In the speech given here, Martin used the phrase 'If we are wrong' many times. Many speech-makers repeat a word or phrase three times to drive their message home.

Victory and backlash

The Montgomery bus protest continued throughout the winter of 1955. People travelled to work on foot, horseback or by car instead of using the buses. Each week Martin encouraged the protesters, speaking of the importance of campaigning peacefully. He was arrested, fined, jailed and released... and still the protest went on.

The bus campaign soon attracted the attention of newspaper reporters. Martin was becoming known as a leader and a powerful speaker. He was also becoming the target for white racism, receiving a stream of threatening letters and phone calls. On 30 January 1956, Martin was out at a meeting when a bomb was thrown on to his front porch. He rushed home to find Coretta and the baby unhurt.

Martin calming the crowd after his house in Montgomery is bombed on 30 January 1956.

INSPIRATION

In 1954 Martin began a close friendship with black minister and civil rights leader Ralph Abernathy. The two remained lifelong friends, with Abernathy at King's side on most campaigns. Another black leader said King 'trusted Ralph like he trusted Jesus.' Martin himself admitted to Ralph: 'I couldn't do my work if you were not here with me.'

Outside his house, an angry mob of African Americans was confronting a few white policemen and officials, who were looking scared. Violence seemed inevitable, but Martin faced the crowd and held up his hand for silence. 'We cannot solve this problem through retaliatory violence. We must meet hate with love.' The men put away their weapons and went home.

After almost a year, the bus protest ended in victory. The protesters had written to the US Supreme Court, asking it to declare segregation on public buses unlawful.

In November 1956 it did so, ordering the rule to be changed. The next month, Martin, his friend Ralph Abernathy and other leaders took their first **integrated** ride, in which no seats were reserved for black or white people. That night, members of the Ku Klux Klan toured black neighbourhoods in their cars, trying to spread terror. But African Americans simply waved back. The black community had found its self-respect and its leader. Black people would no longer be cowed.

Martin (second row) and Ralph Abernathy (front, right) take the first integrated bus ride in Montgomery, 1956.

WOW!

Martin's words on 30 January spread his fame as a lover of non-violence. A white policeman told a reporter: 'I owe my life to that… preacher, and so do all the other white people who were there.'

The victory of the Montgomery bus protest sparked similar campaigns across the South. Some cities introduced **desegregation,** but many resisted reform. An organisation called the Southern Christian Leadership Conference (SCLC) was formed to co-ordinate the campaigns. King was its first president. Meanwhile his first son, Martin Luther King III, was born.

Martin and the SCLC now had two main aims. One was to end segregation. The other was to urge black people to vote. In theory, voting was open to all Americans. In practice, poor, badly educated people were prevented from voting by local laws that required voters to pay a special tax and to prove they were **literate.** The result was that out of 5 million African Americans of voting age in the late 1950s, only 1.5 million were registered to vote.

Martin was determined to change all this. In 1958 he launched a Crusade for Citizenship, aimed at doubling the number of African Americans who voted in the next national election.

In February 1957 Martin appeared on the cover of the very popular Time *magazine – proof of how his fame had spread.*

All this time, Martin's fame was growing. He wrote a book, *Stride Toward Freedom*, about the Montgomery protest. He was gaining friends, but also enemies. The strongest criticism came not from white racists but from a black Muslim leader called Malcolm X, who did not agree with Martin's ideal of non-violence. Malcolm X believed black people should defend themselves against violence, not 'turn the other cheek'.

In September 1958 Martin was signing copies of his book in a New York bookstore when a black woman with mental health problems attacked him, plunging a knife into his chest. He was rushed to hospital, and spent months recovering after surgeons removed the knife. During this time he and Coretta visited India and prayed at the shrine of Indian leader Mahatma Gandhi.

Indian leader Mahatma Gandhi urged his followers to remain non-violent even if violence was used against them. He helped to win India's independence from Britain.

WOW!

When Martin was stabbed, the knife touched, but did not cut through, a vital artery in his heart. Doctors said he would have died if the weapon had gone an inch deeper – or if he had sneezed before it was removed!

INSPIRATION

Mahatma Gandhi invented the tactic of non-violence when campaigning to win Indian independence in the early 1900s. He also used civil disobedience to press for social change. Martin returned from India convinced that Gandhi's tactics were right.

Standing up for freedom

In the late 1950s the civil rights movement made slow progress. Martin reluctantly gave up his job as a minister in Montgomery to devote more time to the struggle. In 1960 the Kings moved back to Atlanta, where the SCLC was based. Martin again became **co-pastor** at his father's church.

The next major campaign in the struggle for civil rights was launched not by the SCLC but by college students. In February 1960 four students from Greensboro, North Carolina sat down at a segregated lunch counter in a department store and refused to move. This sparked a wave of non-violent sit-ins across the South. The following year, black and white protesters started riding **interstate buses** to fight segregation on public transport. These journeys were called Freedom Rides.

The Freedom Riders faced extreme violence from racists. Several buses were burned, as shown here. Many protesters were beaten up and three were killed.

GRO.

Martin gave both campaigns his full support. In 1960 he was arrested during a sit-in and given a harsh sentence of four months' hard labour. A few months earlier he had met the young, ambitious Democratic **presidential** candidate, John F. Kennedy. Kennedy had realised that Martin's support could be vital in the approaching election. Now, he arranged for Martin's release. This action won over black voters, and helped Kennedy become President in November 1960.

However, Kennedy's victory did not immediately result in progress for black civil rights. In 1963 Martin launched a campaign in Birmingham, Alabama. Birmingham was known as the most segregated city in the South. Its police chief, Bull Connor, was famous for his racist views. He was backed by the state governor, George Wallace. Marches and sit-ins in department stores were organised to protest against segregation. Martin was arrested and thrown in the city jail.

A police photograph of Martin Luther King Jr at a police station in Montgomery, Alabama in 1956.

WOW!

King was not allowed paper to write on in Birmingham Jail. His famous letter was written on scraps of newspaper, paper bags, even toilet paper – anything he could find.

INSPIRATION

In Birmingham Jail Martin wrote a famous letter to answer white churchmen who claimed he was too extreme. 'We have waited for more than 340 years for our constitutional and God-given rights... If the inexpressible cruelties of slavery could not stop us, the opposition we now face will surely fail.' His words became a rallying cry for the civil rights movement.

We shall overcome

By 1963 the civil rights movement was in full swing. In southern America opinion was divided. Some white people fully supported the campaign, but there were also racists in powerful positions, who were determined to keep black people 'in their place'.

In Birmingham, Alabama, the protests continued, but many activists had been jailed. Martin reluctantly allowed children to join in the protests. On 2 May 1963, a thousand children marched through the streets of Birmingham. Bull Connor and his men arrested 900. The next day 2,500 more children appeared. The police chief ordered his men to **disperse** the marchers using high-pressure water hoses, fierce dogs and electric cattle prods. TV cameras recorded these events and sent them around the world.

WOW!

On 5 May 1963, a group of churchmen led a march in Birmingham. Bull Connor ordered his men to turn their hoses on the protestors, but this time they refused, and stood aside to let the marchers by. The tactic of non-violence was paying off at last.

A police dog attacks a young protestor in Birmingham, 1963.

The eyes of the world were now on America. Unrest spread across the South. Demonstrations took place in 100 cities, and 20,000 people were arrested. The jails were full to bursting. In many places violence was directed against the campaigners, and in some cases they fought back. President Kennedy realised he had to act. He called in the army to restore order, and also proposed a Civil Rights Bill to the US **Congress**.

Black campaigners organised a march on Washington to press Congress to pass the bill. It was at this demonstration that Martin made his famous speech: 'I have a dream' (see page 5). The campaign now had widespread support in America and abroad. TV and newspapers broadcast the protesters' message worldwide: 'We shall overcome'.

INSPIRATION

On 11 June 1963, President Kennedy made a speech about the Civil Rights Bill. 'The heart of the question is whether all Americans are to be afforded equal rights and equal opportunities. I shall ask Congress… to make a commitment it has not fully made in this century, to the **proposition** that race has no place in American life or law.'

President Kennedy (third from right) meets civil rights leaders including Martin (second from left) in August 1963. Vice President Lyndon B. Johnson is standing to the right of President Kennedy.

A day in the life of Martin Luther King Jr

Martin Luther King Jr worked incredibly hard all his life. He was often up before dawn and still working long after dark. His busy schedule was carefully organised so that he could meet as many demands on his time as possible.

Martin spent a lot of time away from home, at marches, demonstrations and meetings. He often worked while travelling, preparing speeches and discussing the way forward with other leaders. The civil rights movement was always short of money, so Martin spent a lot of time fund-raising. He also had to respond to a steady stream of requests from local and national groups, asking him to speak and support their cause. When he appeared in public, he was often besieged by reporters or by ordinary people wanting advice or autographs.

WOW!

In 1963 alone Martin Luther King Jr travelled an incredible 440,000 km (275,000 miles). In the same year he made 350 speeches – nearly one for every day of the year.

Martin Luther King Jr ducks, having been hit on the head by a rock at a protest in Chicago.

When not on the road, Martin had to fulfill his duties as a minister, preaching sermons and helping the community. He loved to be with his family, but there was very little time for relaxation. Coretta once told a reporter: 'We like to read and to listen to music, but we don't have time for it. We can't sit down to supper without somebody coming to the door.'

Since the mid-1950s Martin had lived under a constant threat of danger. He regularly received death threats, and on demonstrations it was not unusual for him to be pelted with stones and bottles. When speaking at meetings, there was always a risk he would be shot at. It took great courage to stand up to the threat of violence, day after day. There was also the risk of being arrested. Martin was regularly treated roughly by police and prison officers. However, prison was at least relatively peaceful. Here Martin had the chance to think, write and plan his next move.

Martin and Coretta at home with their daughter Yolanda and their son Martin Luther King III in 1960.

HONOURS BOARD

By 1963, Martin and Coretta had four children: Yolanda was born in 1955, followed by their first son, Martin Luther King III, in 1957. Then came Dexter Scott in 1961 and Bernice Albertine in 1963. Martin loved his children, but his busy schedule prevented him from spending as much time with them as he would have liked to.

Fresh battles

On 22 November 1963, President Kennedy was killed by a gunman. Martin grieved along with the rest of America, saying that the killing reflected a growing 'climate of hate'. Martin also feared for his own life, telling Coretta it was unlikely he would live to reach 40.

The new president, Lyndon B. Johnson, urged Congress to pass the Civil Rights Bill in Kennedy's honour. It duly became law in June 1964. The Jim Crow laws were **dismantled** throughout the South.

HONOURS BOARD
Nobel Prize winner:

In 1964 Martin Luther King Jr was awarded the Nobel Peace Prize. At 35 years old, he was the youngest person ever to receive this honour. At the prize-giving ceremony Martin made a moving speech about the distrust and hatred that existed in America. 'We have learned to fly the air like birds and swim the sea like fish, but we have not learned the simple art of living together like brothers.'

Martin Luther King Jr displays his Nobel Peace Prize medal in Oslo, Norway, in December 1964.

Segregation was now illegal. However in many southern cities, African Americans were still discouraged from voting, and made up only a small percentage of voters. Nowhere was this more true than in the town of Selma, Alabama, where just 350 of 15,000 African Americans were registered to vote. Selma's police chief, Sheriff Jim Clark, was a known racist, and some of his deputies were in the Ku Klux Klan. George Wallace was still the state governor.

Martin decided to focus the drive for voter registration on Selma. In January 1965 he joined a demonstration and was arrested. On 7 March, campaigners set out to march from Selma to the state capital Montgomery, to **petition** George Wallace. Martin could not be there. Sheriff Clark called out state troopers and deputies to halt the march. They set upon the peaceful demonstrators with whips and clubs wrapped in barbed wire. 140 were seriously injured. Again, there was widespread outrage when the news became known. To calm the situation, President Johnson rushed the Voting Rights Bill through Congress. It became law in August 1965 – another victory for the civil rights movement.

TOP TIP

Martin was now an expert speaker, skilled at moving people with his words. Use these tips to plan your own speech: note down the points you want to make as headings. Don't write out every word. Practise your speech in a mirror or in front of your family or your friends.

Martin Luther and Coretta Scott King lead a march from Selma to Montgomery in March 1965.

Widening the struggle

By 1965, discrimination against black Americans and other minorities was illegal. However throughout America, there was still little equality between black and white people. In both the North and South, African Americans lived in the worst housing, in poor **ghettos**, and were poorly educated. Black people and other minorities did the worst-paid jobs, if they had work at all.

A portrait of Martin Luther King Jr, taken in 1966.

In the hot summers of 1964 and 1965, hardship and poverty led to rioting in black neighbourhoods in some cities. The riots were started by black activists who did not share Martin's belief in non-violence. Members of a movement called Black Power believed that violent rebellion was needed to overthrow white control in America.

Martin remained completely against violence and felt that these protests were wrong. However, he understood why black people were angry. He became convinced that the whole American economy needed to be reformed, so that all citizens had a more equal share in the country's wealth.

WOW!

Between 1955 and 1967 Martin Luther King Jr was arrested 120 times, and spent many months in jail.

In 1965 the Kings moved to Chicago, Illinois, to campaign against poverty. They took rooms in a poor district in this northern city to experience the hardships faced by most black people. Martin was planning a Poor People's march on Washington that would unite poor people of all races. Meanwhile he campaigned for jobs and better employment laws and against poverty in Chicago. However, these issues were so broad and far-reaching it was difficult to get results.

Martin was also questioning American policy abroad. In 1967 he spoke out against the Vietnam War, which had been going on for a decade. Since 1964, American involvement in the war had **intensified**. Martin's speech about Vietnam attracted criticism from all sides, including from the newspapers and President Johnson. Still Martin believed it was right to stand up for what he believed in, even if it made him unpopular.

TOP TIP

Sometimes it can be hard to stand up for what you believe in, especially if it makes you unpopular. Your chances of succeeding will be much greater if, like Martin, you stay calm, non-violent and true to your beliefs.

CHILDREN ARE NOT BORN TO BURN

*Martin Luther King Jr at an anti-Vietnam War demonstration in New York. The boy's poster refers to the American policy of dropping a substance called **napalm**, which causes burning, on enemy villages in Vietnam.*

Death and legacy

Martin regularly received death threats. By 1967 Malcolm X and a number of other political leaders had been **assassinated**. Martin believed he might be next, but even that didn't stop him campaigning courageously.

In March 1968 Martin travelled to Memphis, Tennessee to lead a march for employment rights. The march set out, but Martin called it off after a group of black youths started breaking windows and looting. The police arrived and a riot broke out. Martin returned to Atlanta, but a week later, he was back in Memphis to lead another march.

On 3 April, Martin made a speech in which he spoke of the 'promised land' of equality, and also seemed to predict his own death. The next evening he was standing on the balcony of the **motel** where he was staying when he was hit by a **sniper's** bullet. He was rushed to hospital but died within the hour. He was 39 years old.

INSPIRATION

On 3 April 1968, Martin seemed to predict he would die before achieving everything he was fighting for. 'We've got some difficult days ahead. But it doesn't really matter with me now. Because I've been to the mountaintop... And I've looked over. And I've seen the Promised Land. I may not get there with you. But I want you to know tonight, that we, as a people, will get to the Promised Land.'

Thousands joined Martin's funeral procession as it made its way through the streets of Atlanta on 9 April 1968.

Sixty thousand people attended Martin's funeral in Atlanta. The funeral address was given by his lifelong friend, Ralph Abernathy. Many others also paid tribute to the fallen leader. The closing words of Martin's famous 'I have a dream' speech were carved on his gravestone: 'Free at last. Free at last. Thank God Almighty I'm free at last.'

Martin Luther King Jr spent his life campaigning tirelessly for civil rights and equality. He excelled as a speech-maker and never gave up his ideal of non-violence. But would the civil rights movement have succeeded without him? By the mid-1950s it was time that segregation was abandoned in the USA. The civil rights movement was inevitable. However, without Martin's guidance the struggle would probably have been a lot more violent. Martin's speeches inspired tens of thousands to join his cause, and his peaceful methods have since been taken up by campaigners all over the world.

This monument to Martin Luther King Jr was unveiled in a park in Washington DC in 2011.

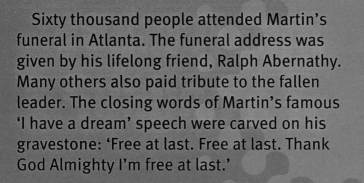

HONOURS BOARD
Remembrance:
In 1983, Martin's birthday became a public holiday in the USA. He is only the third person after George Washington and Christopher Columbus to be honoured in this way.

Have you got what it takes to campaign for a cause?

1) Is there something you believe in passionately, and are you prepared to work to make your dream come true?
a) I feel strongly about things, and I'm prepared to work for what I think is right.
b) I don't mind hard work but I wouldn't say I had a vision.
c) Easy come, easy go is my motto. I don't get too wound up about anything.

2) Have you got the guts and determination to see things through, or do you give up easily?
a) My motto is 'If at first you don't succeed, try and try again'.
b) I don't give up that easily, but I don't believe in trying endlessly when something seems pointless.
c) I tend to cut my losses and give up if I don't get quick results.

3) Are you a natural leader? Can you get others to follow your lead?
a) I don't mind taking the lead if it's something I believe in.
b) I'm a good team player, but not keen to take the lead.
c) I don't think I'm a natural leader. People say I'm bossy if I try to tell them what to do.

4) Have you got the courage to stand by your principles even if it makes you unpopular?
a) I stick to what I believe and try to bring others round to my point of view.
b) I don't mind standing up for something I believe in, but I don't like going it alone.
c) I tend to go with the flow – I don't like to be unpopular.

5) Are you good at public speaking?
a) I never mind standing up and saying my piece in front of a crowd.
b) I have spoken in public, but it makes me nervous.
c) I'm quite shy. The thought of public speaking makes me want to run!

6) Are you good at tactics – do you know when to back off, in order to fight another day?
a) I think out my goal carefully and plan how to get to it. Sometimes that involves backing off.
b) I know what I want, but it's not so easy to know how to get it.
c) It's funny, but I always seem to choose the wrong moment to speak up.

RESULTS

Mostly As: You've got what it takes to be a campaigner: vision, determination and the ability to lead and inspire others. You would be an asset to any cause!

Mostly Bs: You're a good team player, but reluctant to take the lead at present. Your next move could be to join a group that campaigns for something you believe in.

Mostly Cs: You lack the drive and commitment to be a campaigner at the moment, but perhaps you just haven't found the right cause!

Glossary

Artery A main blood vessel.

Assassinate To kill someone.

Boycott To refuse to use or to buy something because of a principle.

Civil disobedience A peaceful form of protest which involves refusing to obey certain laws or pay taxes.

Civil rights The rights of all citizens to be treated equally and have a say in government.

Community A group of people, such as the people living in a neighbourhood.

Congress The law-making part of the American government, made up of the Senate and the House of Representatives.

Desegregation When segregation is removed. (See *Segregation*)

Discrimination Treating people badly, or being prejudiced against them.

Dismantle To take something apart.

Disperse When a group of people separates.

Divinity God or the study of God and religion.

Ghetto A poor part of a city, which is inhabited by people of the same racial group.

Illegal Against the law.

Integrated Not separated, for example, by race.

Intensify To become stronger.

Interstate bus A bus that travels between states.

Literate Someone who can read and write.

Minority A relatively small group of people that is a different race or religion, or speaks a different language, from other groups.

Motel A hotel which is situated on a road, and so can be used by motorists.

Napalm A substance that causes burning when mixed with fuel.

Ordained When someone becomes a minister of the Church.

Pastor A minister in the Church.

Petition To ask for or demand something.

Prejudice A negative judgement about someone or something, formed without knowing the facts.

Presidential Of the President.

Proposition A proposal or suggestion.

Racism Discriminating against people on the grounds of race.

Racist A person who discriminates against people on the grounds of race.

Seamstress A woman who earns her living by sewing.

Segregation Separating people, for example, by race.

Sniper A gunman.

Index